To an American Man,

All my love,

[signature]

12/4/05

Nursery Rhymes

of

The Female Mind

Poetry

by

Gina Minicuci

Photographs by Karle Fried

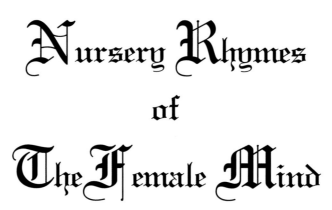

Nursery Rhymes
of
The Female Mind

Poetry by

Gina Minicucci

PUBLISHED BY SYNERGY BOOKS
2100 Kramer Lane, Suite 300
Austin, Texas 78758

For more information about our books, please write to us, call 512.478.2028, or visit our website as www.bookpros.com.

ISBN: 0-9755922-8-9
ISBN: 978-0-9755922-8-1
Library of Congress Control Number: 2005926615

Back cover and author page photographs: Ed Ochal
Photographs: Karle Fried

Preface

"Never sacrifice yourself,
instead always strive to fulfill your dreams."

-Amedeo Modigliani (1884-1920)

There once was a time when every woman had her "place" in the world. This place offered few or no options other than which china to use with what linens or which hat to wear with what dress. All that has changed; today we are liberated. Now not only do we have options, we have confusion, commotion, love and devotion. We are distracted, we are reenacted, we are who we dare to be; and, around every corner, we see opportunities and decisions. We are a species on a mission. We are CEO's, political officers, soccer moms and literary scholars. We are lovers, we are fighters, we are the breadwinners who work in diners. But most of all, we are human. We've loved those we've lost, and lost those we've loved. We wake up every morning, open our eyes, think of the day ahead and stare at the glass ceiling above our beds. We laugh and we cry and wonder why, oh, why we run in place, yet desire so much more space. With all that we are and all that we dare to be, the one thing I ask us to remember is to always strive to fulfill our dreams.

Dedication

 This book of rantings is dedicated to all women who strive to define themselves through all that they are, and in every situation that they seek as independent, self-sufficient, and wise beyond their times, those who challenge who they dare to be, and share with everyone they see their expertise, experience, love and laughter, and will forever and ever … happily ever after.

Acknowledgments

I want to thank my family for all of their support and encouragement (despite their prejudices of loving me). Also, all my supportive friends who have always been there for me and will always be a part of my heart. And, to all who have contributed so much magic and inspiration: Miss K—Your talent made this project amazing; Ed Ochal—You made me gorgeous; John Paul Owles with Joshua Tree Publishing; Michael Brand, my fabulous sound engineer; Taryn Esof and Leilani Garcia, my supermodels; Catherine Ponder for making me camera-ready; and, of course, every man, woman, child and town that has inspired so many words and thoughts throughout my travels. A very special thanks to my partner, agent and friend, Dave Szelap, without whom the distribution of this book would have never been possible.

THANK YOU!

I LOVE YOU

ALWAYS AND FOREVER,

GYPSY BLEU

Contents

"We are Women, hear us roar—
but don't you dare forget
to open our f*****g doors."

Life

Gypsy Fit

I call it a
Gypsy fit,
Pack my travel kit
And can't breathe.
It's time to leave
All that I've built
Behind
In order to find
Something else
To distract me
From myself.
I get so bored
Being in accord
And compliance
With my
Surrounding alliance
All the time.

So I build another
To remind
Me of who I am,
Undefined by any
Description of
Whatever I can
Or cannot do
According to me
And my bicycle
Built for two.
Where are you from?
What do you do?
What's it to you
And your preconceived
Notion
Of grinning and
Spinning and

Falling without
Motion?
What do you care?
Do you really dare
To jump aboard
This bicycle
Built for two?
Can you afford
The time
Or mistake?
Could you take
A leap of faith
And stop
Doing what you do?
What's it going to be?
The world according
To me
Or the world according
To you?

Saturn Returns

Saturn returns
A complete transition
Without moving an inch
I'm changing position.
Something's got to go
Something's got to change
Something's telling me
I've got to rearrange
My points
My intentions
Disregarding any apprehensions.
Saturn returns
Subconscious obsessions
Controlling my mind
Searching to find
My path
My plan.
I've never been a big fan
Of this

Or that
It's all tit for tat.
Without thinking twice
I entice
My instincts
To do what they dare
Wherever they take me
At least, I'll be there.
Saturn returns
Is my excuse for ambition
All I needed was a little
Ammunition.
Ready-aim-fire
It's "Gina for hire"
At least for a while
Until Venus retires

Saturn returns.

Pro-Choice

This is shit
You only hit
After Saturn returns.
It hasn't yet begun
Your candle's not yet burned
You'll only deter the ambition
There's so much ammunition.
So much to see
So much to learn
What it truly is
That really makes you yearn
For desire

For disaster
For happily ever after.
You don't know
Who's to say
You won't
Until that day
When something
Will tell you
It'll be okay
Whichever way
You may sway.

Embracing the Uncertainty

Who, what, when
Will I be?
I'll embrace the uncertainty
And assume
That one day
There will be
No more questions
Or suggestions.
When I can exhale
And tell my tales
Of coast to coast
Failures and successes
Spontaneous second guesses
Unwelcome trespasses
Of reservations

And destinations
And all the temptations
Of the open road
Undoing its code.
My soul playing its toll.
Options, confusion, commotion
Creating some
Magic potion
And with it I shall find
Some piece of mind
Or in due time
It will find me
And finally
Set me free –

I'll embrace the uncertainty.

Confused

What to do
What to do
Who am I supposed
To be?
Only if I knew ...
A writer
A teacher
A philosophical preacher
A professor
An artist
A mother
Or guitarist.
I need to find an answer
I so desire a cure
For all of this uncertainty
Of something
I must be sure.

Just Wondering

Today, tomorrow or never
Will it ever be forever?
Anything
Everything
Nothing or something.
Please, from on my knees,
What, a few days,
months, years
Many fears, many tears
What will's
What wont's
Do's and don'ts
The notion of falling
Without motion
Turning and spinning
I'm grinning
From day to day
I'm on my way.

Lost and Found

Things that I long for
And things that may
Never be
These are my passions
These are me.
Hoping for the hopeless
And desiring the works
A life without hourly
Yet all of the perks
Of fame and fortune
Love and devotion
A house in the hills
And magical potions
Of life with no bills
And of course
Prince charming
With good looks
And his grace
Who comes and goes
According to my taste.
Beauty and paradise
Everywhere around
This is where
I long to be lost
And live
Never to be found.

The Letter

Dear Madness
That surrounds
And hounds me
I feel you
Taste you
Smell you
And deny you
Access to my
World of peace.
You shall cease
To infect me
And direct me
Into your whirl
Of chaos.
I no longer embrace
What you offer.
I now face
One direction
And avert your
Infections
Of upheaval
And dismissal
Of all that I've built
With tenacious intentions.

I won't bare guilt
Or permit
Your infections
I'm here now
And I plan to stay
Wherever I may be
It finally feels okay.
So go away
And let me be,
You've found me
Dear madness
Now I beg of you
set me free.

Denial

Winter is approaching
As quickly as
It left before.
The year has flown by
And with it I deny
All that I have
Seen, done, felt and said
Keeping all privy information
Locked up in my head
Sweetly catalogued
In a simple chaotic order
Creating a fine-lined border
Enabling sanity and beauty
To rise above
This five-foot-four shell
That keeps me together
Or whatever,
The file of denial
Is an ongoing trial.

Tenacity

Frustration is an understatement.
Disappointment surrounds me.
It's all a big game of
"I'm interested, but
Don't bother me."
No shows
Tentative plans
Phone tag
And one-night stands.
I only desire a shot
I'll take whatever
You got.
Bring it on
Bring it on
Show me
What you're not ...
Not afraid
Not betrayed
By love
Or by hope.
Take a chance on me
Is all I ask
Otherwise, I'll be here
Tuggin' on your rope.

The Feminist

I am an example
Somewhat of a sample
Of what today's woman should be
Strong, independent, and wise
Always in disguise
Hiding the true me.
My friends look at my ways
With admiration and praise
Content, alone, without company.
Little do they know
It's all just a show.
I made this choice
So long ago
When I lost my voice
Inside a lovers soul.
I walk tall now
I eat alone
I carry books by

Virginia and Poe
I read in coffee shops
And drink cappuccino
All the while fantasizing
Of my future in Portofino
With my Italian lover
By my side
Enabling me to hide
Behind the title
Of his bride.
Though it's not
Simply love and passion
I desire
But an escape from
"Gina for hire".
Someone give me a break
I can no longer fake
All the pride it takes
To endure

All the coffee shops
And bus stops
People checkin' me out
I'm loaded with
Self doubt
Yet so many aspirations
Please someone deliver me
From temptation
Or I swear I will explode
And turn into a toad
Unless prince charming
Sweeps me off my feet
Negating all that I have
Suffered to beat
Oh the oath of hypocrisy
The tangled webs we weave
Sneakin' up on me
Like a skilled
Guild of thieves.

Destiny's Hand

As long as I live
I will never forgive
Destiny's hold on me
No matter what I try
She will always deny
Any changes I'd like to see
I'm destined to grow old
I'm destined to unfold
Under any situation
Involving heartbreak and misery.
I'm destined without luck
Always just a fuck
Is the story of my life
Or at least seems to be.
Could I be depressed
Despite my intellect?
Has heartbreak finally
Gotten the best of me?
Say it isn't so
Someone let me know
If she might someday consider maybe
Letting me go,
Or at least possibly
Setting me free
Until then,
Destiny's got a hold
Of me.

Raindrops

Pit Pat
Pit Pat
I love the rain
When it sings
Like that
Provoking thought
Evoking soul
It's somber beat
Of rock and roll
It brings me peace
A new lease on life
A little time to
Chill out and
Treat myself right.

Slow it down
Kiss the ground
Smell the air
And feel the despair
For all the rain drops
Everywhere
Dripping from flower petals
And leaves of trees
Growing into puddles
Rippled by the breeze
I stay inside
Dry and warm
Pit Pat
Pit Pat
It's just the calm
Before the storm.

Love

Thank You

Thank you
I sit here while
My mind wanders
To yesterday
And days previous
With you
Laughing and learning
Things new
Times two
Gifts of gentle
Kisses on my forehead
Subliminal thoughts of
Comical connotations
Motivations alike
Fresh fruits and breads
Smilin' eyes, good wine
I visualize
Coastal highways
Fireworks
Creative energy
In shades of
Blues and Greens
I apologize to
The analytical side

And forbid it
To infect
With intellect
The warmth and comfort
Of blisters from
The fun
And sun
That surrounds
I'm found
Though never lost
Without cost
Given one
Magical moment
Of blissful lust
Thank you
Times two
Forever and always,

Gypsy Bleu

43

An Old Friend

You were an aquaintence
of many moons ago
An old friend
that I didn't really know.
We crossed paths
in an unfamiliar land
Shared cocktails and held hands.
You took me to places
I've never seen before
Up the gorge and to the shore.
We hiked and climbed
Wined and dined
For 4 days and 3 nights
It was a blast but something

Wasn't right.
I felt it in the air
And hour before you left
All that we had shared
Was just a memory to be kept.
Despite your casual ways of
planting seeds
Of future plans
You fled from me with my
Heart in your hands.
I never heard from you again
You definitely weren't a friend
Just a momentary lover
Disguised undercover
I could've handled that

Had it been a fact
But you played it otherwise
Like a friend in disguise.
I believed your interest as sincere
I thought I had no reason to fear
It was a first for me to be
Discarded
Like a bad hand you
Bluffed and got what
You wanted.
Now our paths have
Crossed again
Only this time you
Are no longer an old friend
Just a memory gone bad
For I am not one to be had.

Daydreams

I was thinking
Maybe you and me
Could go sit under
A tree
Somewhere.
And dare to share
A thought
Maybe get caught
Up
In one another's
Dreams.
Wouldn't it be nice
To smoke cigarettes
Without regrets
Of the politically correct
To drink coffee

Instead of tea
Just you and me
Under a tree
It would grow
Real slow
And we'd just sit there
Without a care
In the salt water
Air
And watch the sun
Set over the sea
I was thinking that
Would be nice
Just you and me
Under a tree.

False Affections

Presumptuous x-boyfriend
Alienating my time
Assuming it's his dime
That I'm on
Like I care to share
The energy it takes
To recreate all the unfounded
Passion I could fake
Without caution
I take
My time everywhere.
Do I dare?
Tell, say
Spill my guts
In some arbitrary way
Would he listen,

Or just watch my eyes glisten
Tempting the lust
That holds no trust
Simply memories
And erections
With false affections.
Do I dare
Does my past
Guide my ways?
Not a chance
What happens next
Only I will say
You had your day
Just remember it that way
For I am no longer
Your prey.

Patience

To whom it may concern,
I'd like to speak up
And say it's my turn
My turn to be happy
My turn to be loved
My turn to be worshiped
Like the heavens above.
I want someone to
Bring me flowers
And check in on the hour
To ask how my day was
And just care because he does.
I want to walk and talk
With coffee
And hang out at the beach
I want someone
Who will teach

And reach out
Without a doubt
Who will shout
And pout
Tears and joy
But not a little boy
Or just another rock star
Only goin' so far
All I'm askin for
Is a level headed catch
With broad shoulders
And intellect
Who would not dare reject
My heart and my mind
For the sake of
A good time.

Off With the Old, On With the New

Try keepin' it real
You'll know how I feel
You lost somethin'
True
Bleu
Forget you
And your words otherwise
You were only a friend
In disguise.
Your leo, ego,
Whatever you want to call it
Go back to your stage
Your guitar
And your mullet
Just another rock star
Only goin' so far

Before eliminating options
Of fabulous concoctions
Passions and poisons
And tons of emotions.
I was a friend
Who wouldn't dare contend
With your smiles
And trials
Of life and love
Anything and everything
From below
Or above.
Well, whatever
What can I do?
I'm just bein me
And your just bein' you.

One Night Stand

I'm serious
Furiously delirious
The master blaster
Of disaster
Goosebumps and laughter
At the thought of
Happily ever after
However, no matter
Your not into the latter
You got what you wanted
And I am left haunted
With the regrets of a tramp
The one night camp
Could've should've would've
As if it was ever really love
My ego's in despair
But my heart doesn't care
Cause I've learned to beware
Of anyone who dares
To tempt me again
To pretend he's a friend
Who won't offend
My honor
Next time I'll ponder
The question of affection
With a little more
Attention

And hopefully, someday
I'll find perfection.

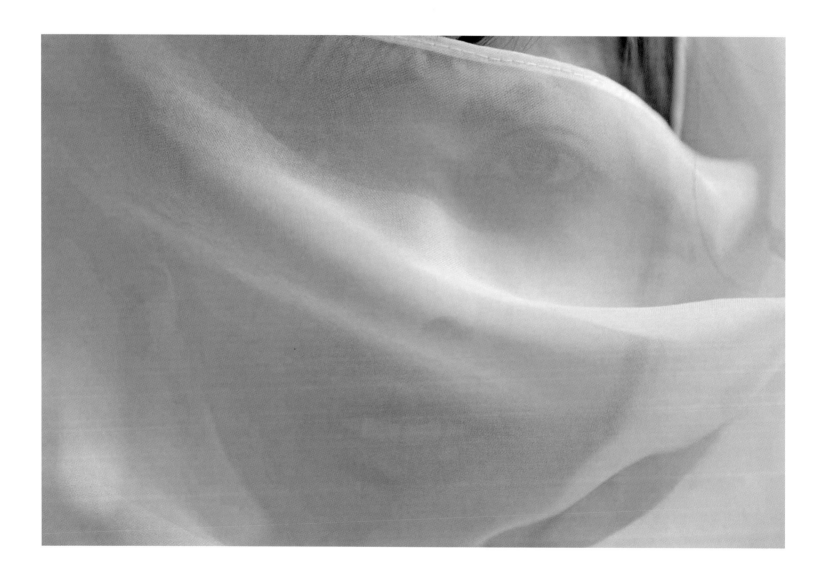

Big Mistake

What was I thinking
Coveting another womans man
What was I drinking
Who the hell do I think I am
Something special
Someone out of the norm
Someone unconventional
Who doesn't have to conform
To morals
Or ethics
Seems to me
Kind of pathetic
Good friends or not
It's time to realize
What I don't got
His love and affection
Are at the attention
Of another's heart
I should walk away now
I should've from the start

It's definitely
Time to depart
From the situation
Lead me not into temptation
But deliver me from evil
I will walk away now
And hopefully
Begin to heal
I'll love him always
With this I'm secure
I've loved him forever
Of this I am sure
Friends we've always been
Friends we'll always be
As for the love of his life
I now know
It will never be me.

Freedom

Alone at last
Alone at last
I should've thought this through
Before I ever asked
For my space
For my freedom
I have it all now
But what if I need him?
Who will change the light bulbs?
Who will tuck me in?
Who will make me dinner?
And tell me I'm to thin.
Will I ever find another
To keep me safe and warm
Or will I always wonder
If we could have
Calmed this storm.

Commitment

Am I capable
Of loving
Without a
Wandering eye
Does my past
Defy
My future desires?
Could I be jaded
My ideals faded
I want a good man
And this he is
It's just whenever
I get what I want
Comes the good-bye
Kiss.
It's a lifestyle curse
Off with the old
And on with the first
Next thing

To come along
Time to move on
Can't let anything
Pass me by
Can't even try
To lay down
Some roots
Retire my boots
Plant some seeds
Or commit my needs
To anyone
Or anything
That might give
Me a ring
Could this be
A fear of commitment
Thing?

Laughter

Cabernet

It is said
A bottle of Red
Gets better with time
Disabling the mind
Creating drama and laughter
Forever after
So satisfying
And gratifying
Nothing lasts forever
So we must remember
The momentary pleasure
Of tears
And of touch
Until it gets to be
Too much
To only savor
Isn't enough

So close your eyes
And visualize
The glass bottle full
Of what came off the vine
Falling and Falling
Down and down
A crash of glass
Into the ground
The beautiful body
Of rich redness everywhere
Without a fear
Or a care
Of consequences
It quenches
My thirst
For disaster
Happily ever after.

San Francisco 2001

The wheels on the
Bus go round
And round
All its' passengers are
Lost and found
As it inches down Market
And pedestrians
Park it
Forever in the way
With signs that say
"Smile, have a nice day"
By the way,
I'm homeless
Could you spare a dollar
While others holler
For down payments on
cheeseburgers
Or a hot cup of coffee
Preying on your sympathy

To set them free
From disaster or perhaps
Bless them with
Happily ever after
The city's fucked
The market's corrupt
Some prepare for the haul
Goin' back to where they came
from
Since the fall
Of the dot-com bomb
Chicago, L.A., and the
Hum drum way
Of life in the burbs
And the day
They were raised.
White picket fences

And present tenses
Leaving behind all
The crazed AIDS victims
And city bums
To live in their door ways
In cardboard boxes
Without much concern
For the big energy crisis.
That's it go home
Everyone get the fuck out
At least maybe then
We can turn the lights on
Without rolling blackouts
Whatever, who cares –
No one was prepared
For population overload
Who could've known
We wouldn't all fit
No shit, it had to happen one day
At least we haven't all fallen in
the bay.

Living for the Art

Inside out
Loaded with self doubt
Livin' for the art
Makes me want to shout
"What the fuck"
I'm shit out of luck
So I just sit and pout.
Sales sucks
It's not in my heart
All I want to do
Is live for the art
That wont pay the bills
Unless it sells
And then it's just cheap thrills
That'll only send me to hell.
I don't know what to do
About my state of mind
As I sit here and dwell
I simply fall behind.
I can't make the cold calls
It's like walking into walls
And hurting my head
To keep getting fed
All the bullshit lines
Like "Now's not a good time,
I'll call you tomorrow"
And then the earth swallows

Swallows them whole
Like spooky little trolls
Who live underground
Only coming out
To play lost and found
It's all about the games
Dropping the right names
Creating the scene
And falling in between
The cracks
It's whacked!
I fail to see the humor
Of this seemingly false future
Will it ever come together
And set me up forever
All I'm askin' is for
A little love
Maybe a little luck
Sent from above
It seems so close
Yet so far away
God give me the patience
To await that day
Awaiting serendipity
It's not that smart
I can't take the self pity
I'm livin' for the art.

Modernism

Oh Plato
You know
So well
"Art is politics"
Were all goin' to hell
We do what we do
In spite of it all
Just tryin' to make sure
It won't go down with the fall
Of this self obsessive culture
Makin' cellular calls
It's so hard to be sure
We can only endure
Or embrace
Pollock, Rothko lead to
Warhol's masterpiece face
Marilyn and Liz
All over the place
Abstract Expressionism
Turned pop
Popularity always prevails
It never fails
To commercialize

All that was once wise.
To all of the ground work
Laid down by Greenberg
And his bureaucratic ways
Suffice it to say
He had his day
Setting aside the inside
Of what history hides
From the eyes
Of society
Of this country
That's oh so free
It's all in philosophy
Tolstoy, Kant, Nietzsche
Just aiming to be
The separate Identity
Of intellect
In effect
Art continues to be
Art for art's sake
And our inner slaves
Shall be freed.

Not to be a Man

We sit over a drink
He talks and
I think
He doesn't understand
He's got all that
He needs
A roof over his head
Slippers under his bed
And a job
That lets' him breathe
I must be high maintenance
Since I need my job
And have no patience
For part time slobs
He doesn't understand
Although he thinks he can
What it's like not to be a man.
He can lose everything
And still have the strength
To sleep in bus stops
And build houses
I'd end up in a shelter
With women beaten
By their spouses

He can walk down the street
And hold his own
If anyone glares
He'd simply groan
I've got to deal
With feeling like
Everyone's meal
Mouth watering men
Staring like I'm
The perfect 10
If I dare glare back
I must be prepared
For an attack
I clutch my mace
Like a squirt in the face
Will ever compare
To the dare
Of desire
For a 44
Ready aim fire –

He doesn't understand
Although he thinks he can
What it's like
Not to be a man.

The Corporate Ladder

Is it possible
Rejected?
I continue unaffected
Your loss
Oh well
I would've been an asset
To your firm of hell
The C.E.O.
Goin' with the flow
Makin' the calls
And fillin' the walls
With contemporary masterpieces
Standin' 8-feet tall
Proving my point
Implementing my plan
Doing whatever I do
Or at least whatever I can

To express all the brilliance
Of thought and artistic beauty
Why just repress
And sell the tooty fruity
The yesterday's news
Of Picasso, Chagall, the Warhol's
Never-ending
Down the endless halls
Of shopping malls
And T-shirts
I'd rather flirt
With the temptation
Of today's inspirations
You'll figure it out
Someday, I pray
In the meantime
I'll be moving forward
While you're stuck
On rewind.

Rêve De Paris

I want to go to Paris
And live among
The French
Parlé français
Tous les jours
Et mon vie vais comménce
I will find my Jean-Pierre
Or maybe Jacques Cousteau
Parlé Français tous les jours
And live life on the go
Faire la bise
Faire la bise
Poésie
Et café
Les musées
Les musées
Je voudrais vivre
Avec les Français.

Poll Position

Do you ever feel
Like your playing
In traffic?
One wrong move
The results could
Be tragic
Stop on red
Go on green
And don't forget
The yellow
In between
This means caution
Some sort of warning
That should've told you
Not to get up
This morning
But you just ignored it
Just drove right through
Cause whatever happens
Could never happen to you
But it could
And it would
Or it can
And it will.
I wouldn't play in traffic
But if you must
Then stay very very still

Happy Hour

Sitting in the bar
It's Friday
Happy hour
Six of us total
Simpsons have the stage
I turn the pages
Of this silly little book
While others look
And then away.
No ones got
Much to say
The end of the day
They sit and pray
To the bartender
To render
Up her concoctions
Of never-ending options
Of how the weekend
Will begin.
Something's got to happen
Who will be the one to win
The game of 8 ball
In the corner
The fat man
Or the thin?

Consultation

Paxil, PMDD
Prozac, Zyban
Cause it's not
Really me
It's hormones
Rejections
A chemical imbalance
With some minor infections
I do what I can
And try not
To be me
I do things like tan
Wear platforms
And drink tea.
I think I feel taller
It's working maybe,
I'm definitely not smaller
Unless I'm barefoot
You see.
A skeptic, eclectic
Paranoid Schizophrenic
Whatever it is
I swear it's
Genetic.

New Years Resolution

Happy New Year
To days on their way
I'm gonna live this one right
Starting today
I'm gonna live out loud
Stand out in crowds
Say what I want
And do what I say
I'm gonna find the
Man of my dreams
Fit into my favorite jeans
Travel across all seas
Learn every romance language
And fall to my knees
At the foot of DAVID
And the Roman cathedrals
Who's gonna stop me
From goin' mid-evil
This is gonna be the year
Where I dismiss
All my fears
And be everything I want
Despite what I'm not
I'm gonna learn to
Play the guitar
And become a
One hit wonder
Rock star.

After Thoughts

I wrote this collection over a period of about three years. I was in my late twenties, trying to find, lose, or define myself through my own experiences as well as the experiences of others, including: friends, foes, strangers, and lovers. Whenever I become overwhelmed with myself in challenging situations, I write and write until I can make some sense of my emotions, my surroundings, and all of my losses and findings.

There came a time when I noticed I wasn't alone. Every time I turned a corner, I found someone else with a similar disorder. I began to share my words in both personal and public situations. My rhymes of thoughts were so well received, I gained praise as well as many confrontations.

I started to feel that my audience was somewhat deceived. My pen is my genius, so to take all the credit became difficult to conceive. Hence came my pen name Gypsy Bleu, given to me by a friend who knows me through and through. I am told however, that I must take some credit since this book is now published and I can never regret it.

My inspirations are derived from the world around me, all of its' people, and all of its' entirety. Special acknowledgements must go to those who wrote before me; unprecedented poets such as Octavio Pas, Ani Difranco, Virginia Wolf, and all who have floored me.

About the Author

Gina Minicuci (A.K.A. Gypsy Bleu) was born in 1972, in the suburbs of Detroit, she's been to many universities, and lived in many cities. She has a bachelor's degree of interdisciplinary studies in Fine art, cultural anthropology, and world literature. Currently, she is working toward a master's degree in art history. She is a member of The International Women's Writing Guild, Poetry Slam Inc, as well as Declare yourself spoken work artists. After many years of trials and travel, Gina is living and writing in Ferndale, MI.

About the Photographer

Karle earned her first bachelor's degree in interdisciplinary studies with emphasis in anthropology and international relations from Michigan State University. She also studied overseas at Tel Aviv University. Karle received a second bachelor's degree in 2004 from California college of the arts in photography. She is currently working as a free lance photographer in the Bay area.

Men

Women

People

INDEX OF PHOTOGRAPHS
BY KARLE FRIED